INSIDE MY OWN SKIN

INSIDE MY OWN SKIN

A Personal Narrative

BY

Guillaume de Fonclare

Translated from the French by Yves Henri Cloarec

Hanging Loose Press
Brooklyn, New York

Dans ma peau © 2010 by Editions Stock.
English translation © 2014 by Yves Henry Cloarec

Published by Hanging Loose Press, 231 Wyckoff Street,
Brooklyn, New York 11217-2208.

www.hangingloosepress.com

Printed in the United States of America
10 9 8 7 6 5 4 3 2 1

Cover art: Courtesy of the Australian War Memorial
Frank Crozier, *The Mud of Desolation*, 1918, oil on canvas, 50.8 x
61 cm, ART00211

Cover design: Marie Carter

ISBN 978-1-934909-39-3

Library of Congress cataloging-in-publication available on
request.

Inside My Own Skin is the third annual winner of the Loose
Translations Award, sponsored jointly by Hanging Loose
Press and the MFA Creative Writing and Literary Translation
Department of Queens College, City University of New York.

Glory has furrowed illustrious streaks
Upon the fearless face of this great horseman
Whose never-humbled brow is weathered
By the tan of war and torrid suns.

—José Maria de Heredia, *Les Trophées* (1893)

My body is a straitjacket. I am a prisoner of the dregs of my bones and flesh. I struggle to walk, to speak, to write, to move these muscles that slash at me constantly. My brain rehashes monotonous refrains; I no longer see my children's smiles or the tender gaze of the one I love; all I see are these hands that shake, these arms that struggle to bring food to my mouth, and these legs that buckle under the weight of a body grown too heavy. I have become nothing more than an uncomfortably seated man who thinks ceaselessly, and, though I once liked this body, I have grown to hate it—from now on we will share living quarters, but it will always have the last word. I have accepted this notion only because I do not have a choice.

There was no accident; no violence caused this state of affairs. It is merely the result of an intimate cruelty of which I am both perpetrator and victim. The origins of this egocentric torture remain a dark secret. I would so much have wished to be able to put a name to this pain, but the affliction from which I suffer has no name. It is one among so many of those orphan diseases, those systemic syndromes, auto-immune diseases, dysfunctions and disorders "of unknown etiology." It is a mystery, and no doctor is in a position to say what form its final outcome will take, nor even when; nor what will be the signs of this feared departure, if indeed the affliction takes me to that point. As a result, I monitor the signs of my slow deterioration, trying not to give in, not to adopt the fatalistic attitude which might accelerate the process.

There had been some tenuous early signs: tingling at the finger-tips, stealthy cramps in the arms and legs, diffuse spasms. I was then thirty-five. At thirty-seven, I started limping. At thirty-eight, I bought a cane. In that same span of time, I graduated from aspirin to morphine and then on to prescriptions with unpronounceable names. Today, everything is in the dosage: too much medication and I am a vegetable; not enough and I cry from the agony. There are very few words that describe the spectrum of my pains: From dulled to sharp, from generalized to localized, they meld into one overarching unit—The Pain. Little by little, I insulate myself within the inability to communicate sensation—which soon becomes an inability to express emotions. Without noticing it, I have distanced myself; the space between me and other people has expanded; my condition has imprisoned me in a situation from which I can no longer escape. Even in my own eyes, I have become so different that I am now some "other," a creature fixated on its agony, growling in pain as it wildly swats away a gesture that had been meant to comfort. Lying down on a bed in the dark is the only alternative to nothingness—a nothingness I have often considered, an idea that softly insinuated itself into my thoughts as one option among others. Eventually I came to see it as the one option that could deliver me from both body and mind. As a result of living everything so intensely, I grew to not want to live at all. I eventually recaptured the will to live, but the memory of this waywardness, and all the hope and despair that accompanied it, is now ingrained in me.

I no longer complain; I no longer speak of the iciness in my hands, or the sun that burns my palms, of the daggers that stab in stealth at night, the stifled cries or the ones I can no longer stifle. Now, there are only outings in which I cannot participate, and I do not even show my bitterness at noticing that my absence from these has become the norm; any activity requiring effort distances me from everything:

I am no longer invited, they make do without me. There is nothing unfair about this. If someone were to ask me, I would answer no: I can't do it; no, I can't any more. I am altogether in that space; now on, I exist somewhere between who I think I still am and who I have become.

To other people—those whose lives do not center on the sick patient—I am, as of four years ago, the director of the Historial, the Museum of the Great War in Péronne, in the Somme Valley. There, I rub shoulders with the ragged, the maimed, the crippled, the dismembered, the disappeared, the mangled, and the broken-face veterans of the "Great War." I am the most living of all these ghosts. Had I been alive seventy years ago, I could have passed for one of them: a great wounded, great decorated, great survivor. But my wounds are not from war; I have been spared the combat, the hand-to-hand, the litany of bombs, screams, fears and anguish. I have been spared the terror of an assault. My hospital is not theirs and, when I am there, I do not hear whimpers other than mine; there are none of the smells and sounds that might make me vomit. Mine is a struggle in vain: From my sacrifice there will be no victory, and the rampart of my body protects neither family nor comrades; I defend no ideal—I merely feel pain, nothing more.

The bodies that surround me crisscross, intertwine and meld. Bodies of my loves: wife and children; farther out, the bodies which carry me and accompany me, friends and colleagues; farther still, bodies of strangers, visitors, tourists, collectors; and finally, there is the multitude of bodies—arranged, aligned, organized or dispersed, all ingested by this land that each year spews up its quota of artillery shells, corpses and rusted relics—the bodies that proceed in the funeral march trailing along behind the more than four hundred and twenty military cemeteries of the Somme.

***

If you follow the path downslope from a thicket of maritime pines, the path that meanders between the grass-covered dig-sites and what remains of bomb craters, you will find the seven hundred graves of the Railway Hollow Cemetery. Beyond this small cemetery is a vast plain covered by fields of grains, beets and potato. If not for the white steles and the ironic juxtaposition of serene beauty with chaos, this strange place would not be unlike the countryside of my youth. Most of the soldiers entombed here were part of the "Pals Battalions. England did not resort to conscription until 1917. Until that time, the British Army relied on the good will of civilians who joined voluntarily, usually in groups—by factory, by neighborhood, or by sports-club affiliation. As a consequence of the British Army being thus constituted, these "pals," all belonging to the same units, would die together, as one after the other of their offensives was decimated by machine-gun fire, a rain of shrapnel or a hail of artillery. Within a three-mile radius of Railway Hollow are twelve cemeteries of the British Commonwealth and one French. Some contain only a few graves; others, several thousand.

The markers on Commonwealth graves are all identical: at the center a cross; at the top, the regimental insignia; under the insignia and the cross, the date of death and age; and at the very bottom, some space reserved for the family to custom engrave an epitaph if they so wished. The nameless corpses are "Known unto God" or "A soldier of the Great War."

At the Railway Hollow Cemetery, the stele of the soldier A. Goodlad bears an inscription that he belonged to the York and Lancaster Regiment and that he died July 1st, 1916 at the age of twenty-six. Goodlad's family added the following inscription: "the French are a grand nation worth fighting for"—a quote from a letter written to his mother by the soldier Goodlad just a few weeks earlier. Ever since I discovered that epitaph, I no longer joke about the *Rosebifs* and I watch rugby matches with a neutrality which to some appears close to indifference, if not betrayal. Yes, even in the face of British chauvinism, I remain unvexed; for, on that July 1st 1916, when soldier Goodlad died so that the great French nation might live, sixty thousand soldiers of the Commonwealth—Brits, Scots, Welsh, Irish, Canadians, Newfies, South Africans, Australians and Kiwis—were put out of action in less than four hours. Of the sixty thousand casualties, twenty thousand killed. The 20th century failed to remember July 1st 1916; it is, however, still to this day the bloodiest day in the entire history of the British Army.

It is two years since I have been to the Railway Hollow Cemetery. The road there is dangerous by car, impassible by wheelchair. Once you reach the gate to the park, you have to cross its breadth, and confronting that hill has become quite difficult for me. Nonetheless, I want to attempt the crossing one last time, as I want to hold on to the feeling that I still control events; I want to separate myself from the places to which I used to go, in full awareness that this is the last time. I will feel the shadows of the pine trees fall upon me, and I will know that this visit will quiet my anxiety, that the peaceful vision of the stone steles will help me feel my own pain with less acuteness and more compassion toward myself. I will sit on the low brick wall which borders the cemetery and I will cry for all these men, too young and too numerous. Then, I will leave, alive, taking with me the memory of each one of them.

***

I was on my way to Limoges when, as the train crossed the dense forests of the Morvan, I became aware of the odd habit I have of peering into the underbrush—quite a single-minded habit indeed, since it forces me to search in the Morvan for something which cannot possibly be there. In the Somme, there are many woods and forests which—being in the area where the front lines used to be—still show some scars of the Great War: old trenches and bomb craters never quite filled back to ground level. I search for these scars as one might peer into an old friend's face for the trace of a twenty-year-old wound, the now barely visible sign of a misfortune once completely shared together.

Now that I almost never walk any more, I pursue my quest from behind the windshield of my car where, because of the speed, each hedge takes the shape of a bunker, a path that of a trench, a rosebush that of a stretch of barbed wire. There was only one occasion on which I did discover, in the thick undergrowth of a forest of oak and birch, the pits and bumps of a battlefield. It was there in Péronne, on Mont Saint-Quentin to be exact, behind the tiny church of Ste. Radegonde (where once stood the abbey of the same name) that a British friend of mine took me to "Radomir Alley" as the soldiers had nicknamed it, the German trench that blocked access to Mont Saint-Quentin on the heights overlooking Péronne. This trench was captured by Australian troops early on the morning of August 31st , 1918, then recaptured that night by the Germans, and finally retaken by the Australians on September 1st, thus opening the way for the liberation of what was left of a Péronne in ruins. Here, on the slopes of Mont Saint-Quentin, just below the skin of grass and plants, those shallow pits and bumps eroded by the years sweat out a past that is everywhere present.

I took Alan Griffin, the Australian Minister for Veteran Affairs on a tour of these woods. He was a dynamic and energetic minister if ever I met one (I note in passing that in Australia, Veteran Affairs is an important post). He was accompanied by General Stevens, his chief of staff. Their clothes sullied by mud, their shoes heavy with clay, fighting thorns and bushes, they struggled to follow the maze of Radomir Alley. Then, having climbed over the top of the parapet, the minister listened in silence as the general explained the course of the battle. We contemplated the plain before us: It was pock-marked by lighter-colored halos left by explosions that had heaved up from below the surface the chalk which then spread in a whorl of white petals onto the black topsoil. Some zigzags, now less defined and greying, suggested other trench lines. At that moment, I had the feeling that we were the uninvited ghosts, we who were surveying a field of battle now buried under the accumulation of ninety years: a few inches of dirt.

In 1993, a group of Australians came to Péronne to celebrate the seventy-fifth anniversary of that city's liberation. Several veterans—all in their nineties—were among them, and none of them had seen France since 1918. To insure their well-being, and to avoid the possibility of any excessive behavior, the Australian government assigned to each veteran an orderly—a cadet from the Duntroon Royal Military College, the Australian equivalent of West Point. It all began rather poorly right from the first night: The veterans managed to elude their young guardians, who searched for many hours before they located their venerable old-timers hanging onto the rail at a local bar, and pretty much inebriated. The cadets received a memorable tongue lashing, and the veterans were politely requested to be on their best behavior the rest of the trip.

Several ceremonies were scheduled for September 1st in Mont Saint-Quentin. At the close of the morning's commemorations, the City of Péronne hosted a cocktail party for the Australian delegation. One of the cadets, worn out by the sleepless nights devoted to supervising his "protégé," had a momentary lapse of attention—some even said he dozed off. Of course the moment he came to, he found himself alone; the veteran he was chaperoning had vanished. You can imagine the terror that gripped the young man as the minutes passed and he visualized his military career disintegrating, while he searched in vain. He saw himself being demoted below the rank of private just as he caught a glimpse of a wobbling silhouette heading towards downtown Péronne; a silhouette that hurried its pace upon realizing it had been spotted. The distance between them was still sizable when the old man stopped at an intersection, sat down on the curb and pulled out an object from his pocket. Quite worried by this unexpected halt, the cadet—who had anticipated a far more hectic chase—sped up to a jog and then a frantic sprint as he noticed that his ward had launched into a soliloquy; was his military career to be so prematurely ended in France because a rebellious old-timer had suddenly become senile? Out of breath, the young man stopped in front of the veteran and was about to curse him out when, silencing him with a raised right hand, the old man reached into his parka with his left and pulled out a can of beer, which he offered to the cadet, gesturing him to sit down. And then, to the memory of a comrade—a man whose name meant nothing to the young cadet—he offered up a toast.

Another Australian story, about two of the soldiers who among so many others launched the September 1st assault on Radomir Alley: Having penetrated the German defenses, they made their way toward the city center under the indiscriminate hail of both enemy and friendly artillery. These two had been fighting together since joining up in 1915 with the Second Division of ANZAC, the Australian and New Zealand Army Corps. They had survived the battle of Gallipoli in the Dardanelles, the Somme offensive in Passchendaele and the German offensive of March 1918. A piece of shrapnel put an end to their joint destiny. The unscathed one promised the wounded one that they would soon drink a beer together, that there was no need to worry, that this was nothing, that all would be well. One can imagine the grimaced smile of the wounded man; one can imagine the entire scene. They never saw each other again; the wound was fatal. I was told the survivor's name was Robert Comb. I was also told that this story has been exaggerated with every retelling. I heard this story in Péronne as it was told by an Australian addressing seven hundred of his countrymen who had come from Australia to commemorate the ninetieth anniversary of ANZAC Day, that astonishing April 25th, which commemorates both the Battle of Gallipoli on April 25, 1915 and the Battle of Villers-Bretonneux of April 25, 1918; the former as horrendous a defeat as the latter was a glorious victory. At six foot seven, I towered over the audience and I could clearly see this hushed crowd, these fourteen hundred eyes riveted on the stage and the storyteller, on Robert Comb and his companions. From a distance of ninety years, we stared at each other without seeing each other, disparate silhouettes communing in history through the tiny stories, the little histories that are insignificant—and thus all the more moving.

There was another Australian who, seeing the cane and the limp of the director of a museum he assumed to be military, thought I might be a veteran of the First Iraq War of 1991. I explained I wasn't a veteran, just a man with an ailment. My pains have no connection to machine gun fire, mines or shrapnel. I have exhibited no courage under fire and, even if I am none the better off for that, I am glad of it.

***

Vickers, 500 rounds a minute. Maxim, 500. Saint-Étienne, 500. Hotchkiss, 500. Chauchat, 400. A wall of bullets caterwauling as it advances at twice the speed of sound; these are the machine guns; dozens, hundreds, of front-line machine guns. Out of the thousands of projectiles hurtling towards you, how many will hit you? And what have you to offer up? Your arm? Your torso? Your leg? A jaw? How do you get up on your feet for that first charge? And how do you do it for a second time? The wounded howl, shells explode, men leap from foxhole to foxhole, and in the trenches they clutch at each other with knife, club or bayonet in hand. How do you do that?

There is more than a world of difference between them and us. That war, so modern and yet so archaic, is the war of a different century. We can no longer understand the reasons that prompted these men to keep going, to climb out of a trench and, under a hail of fire and steel, cross the dozen or hundred yards separating them from the next trench. We are indeed no longer part of that same world. There can be no "Duty of Memory," as we no longer remember, and as it is impossible to recall that which is unimaginable. Thus, we must teach, educate, and demand of ourselves a commitment to a duty to history.

In the photographic records of the Australian War Memorial there is a 1916 picture of one Sergeant Robert Potter posing in a village of the Somme with a veteran of the Franco-Prussian War of 1870. Without a doubt, both men had the feeling they belonged to the same world, the same times: an old-timer and a young'un. Yet, these two conflicts are as different from each other as are, say, the battles of Crécy[1] and Stalingrad. The Verdun Plateau is the witness of how horrendously "new" the First World War was: nothing comparable to the Battle of Sedan or the Siege of Belfort[2]. Even so, the generals of the Great War remained convinced

---

1   *Battle of Crécy* (or *Cressy* in English) during the 100 Years War; 26 August 1346

2   *Sedan and Belfort: two battles of the Franco-Prussian War of 1870*

that the only good fight was on horseback or in a bayonet charge; that the ultimate goal of any offensive was breaking through the enemy line, which would then allow the massive charge by mounted troops. As a result, up until 1918, entire regiments of cavalry stood at the ready, waiting in vain for a chance to engulf the enemy.

When viewing the archival movies, if you merely slow down the projector's speed, that eccentric mechanical staccato of scarecrow movements takes on a more natural pace. At that moment, those images which elicited smiles now take on a tragically human dimension. Those women with their corseted wasp waists are our grandmothers; those mustachioed braggarts, those fragile silhouettes fading into the smoke, our grandfathers. Yes, it is indeed our grandfathers who fought there, who cowered in that trench for days or weeks (or was it hours? It makes no difference). For us, merely imagining ourselves there for fifteen minutes panics us: the mud that sticks to everything, that sullies everything; the dust you swallow, the stifling heat, the piercing cold, the stench of urine, excrement and guts; and the rats, my Lord, the rats, the ticks, the clap . . . we had reached the point where it was possible to doubt that we all belonged to the same species, the human race. The pictures remind us that it was indeed our grandfathers, fellow humans, who fought here, and in those conditions.

A world unraveled between 1914 and 1918. Upon its ruins we rebuilt something else. The Second World War definitively sealed our divorce from the early 20th century, which—as far as our children are concerned—will soon belong to the medieval era. To which world do I belong? No matter what anyone says, I am neither a persistence of memory, nor a witness to history; and to use such grandiose terminology would be a form of lying. I merely feel I stand beside those soldiers whose unsteady gait and jerky movements were captured by the newsreel cameras at the rear-echelon hospitals. Of course, I reason with myself and I put each one of us back in his rightful place, each in his own world. Nevertheless, something tells me I belong as much to one as I do to the other. And yet, you and I share nothing in common with these men. They are not heroes, nor are they cowards; they are merely citizens of another time in another world. Yes, they suffered just as we suffer—the stab of a bayonet is still a bayonet's stab; a limb torn from the body is still a torn limb; but we no longer face each other in uniforms: it is no longer a question of green against blue or Lebel rifles versus Mausers. In our time, we have *low-intensity conflicts* and the threats are *elusive*; military strikes are *surgical* with *low collateral damage*, even if some of the weapons are *of mass destruction*. We no longer have civilians and soldiers: we speak instead of *combatants* and *non-combatants*, of *hostiles* and *friendlies*. And if a single soldier dies, the entire Nation mourns; we have come to see the death of one military man as an unacceptable loss.

In those days, no one would have talked about *Post-Traumatic Stress Disorder* or *Collateral Damage*, and yet everyone fully understood the effects on body and soul caused by an artillery barrage, a chemical attack, or the stench of decomposing flesh rising from mass graves or by chunks of both man and beast splattered on a uniform. Some lost their minds in the silence of a hospital or in the chaos of a court-martial. Others might put an end to misfortune by pressing their big toe on the trigger of the long-barreled rifle placed in the mouth. The desire—the temptation—to no longer suffer is fulfilled by death; and yet death is the definitive suffering. What, then, is the alternative? I do not know. The ghosts of the Great War whirl around me; they whisper words I cannot understand; they speak to me of battles I have not known; an aggressive odor, camphorated and acrid, wafts from the soil beneath my steps; the sky tumbles tight-knit tears. I walk a minute more and then am still and silent. All of these words echo within me, quiet clamors that slash at my heart, and the figures in black and white that twist and gyrate on the screen belong to men like me. Two arms, two legs, a torso, a head. Sometimes one of the crucial elements may be missing; but they are men nonetheless.

Robert Potter must have survived the war, as his name appears nowhere in the database of the Commonwealth War Graves Commission—the entity entrusted with the maintenance of all Commonwealth military cemeteries. This absence from those rosters means that he neither died nor disappeared at any time during the war years. He must have returned to Australia, his farm or job, his wife or parents. It might be some of his great-grandchildren I meet in the museum; others question me and, with a century's worth of bottled-up emotion, they cry facing the grave marker of the reluctant hero who bears their ancestor's name. In fact, for many, there has been no Armistice, and the rebuilding has only been a facade: the Great War lives on, cradled in many a sofa, those where one stretches out to bemoan softly the too painful past.

***

Only on one occasion did I have the opportunity to witness the unearthing of human remains, to discover firsthand what the earth does to a body over the course of ninety years. To be precise, I should say two bodies: the hand of one man once held the bayonet which he had plunged into the chest of the other, while the latter had thrust a dagger into the former's throat. They had both tumbled into a trench that an artillery shell explosion then collapsed back on top of them. The vision of these two skeletons skewered one to the other will never leave me. One was a French officer (he had a pistol and watch), the other, as one might expect, a German. The drama had unfolded near Chaulnes, in the Somme, most probably around March 1918. The Military Graves Commission came to remove the remains of the Frenchman and the Volksbund Deutsche Kriegsgräberfürsorge came for those of the German. If it had been up to me, I would have left them together; but I was told such things just aren't done. The scowls when I made the suggestion led me to understand this was just unimaginable; they had spent ninety years together—it was simply out of the question that they should spend one more day that way.

We find corpses all the time; dozens each year. As soon as a construction site of some size is established, provisions are made for such a possibility and its hazardous corollary, the unexploded shell. During the construction of the A29 motorway between Reims and the coast of Picardy, the British Army dispatched a battalion of infantrymen for the duration of the excavation phase, so that proper military honors could be paid to the remains of Her Gracious Majesty's soldiers. Indeed, in most cases, it is still possible to determine the bones' nationality—a swatch of fabric, an insignia, a flask, a medallion, a photo; at other times, less often, it is even possible to discover the unit to which he belonged; in very rare cases, thanks to a dog-tag, we can know the name.

Some countries resort to more detailed investigations than others. Australia routinely employs DNA testing when they cannot otherwise determine identity. Such was the case for the grave found in 2008 in Fromelles, near Calais, which contained the remains of some two hundred Brits and two hundred Aussies. As a rule, Commonwealth nations are very attentive to how the remains of their soldiers are treated: they were never known to resort to a mass ossuary. Even if it is a single tibia that is recovered, it is given its own burial; a soldier of the Commonwealth might therefore have multiple gravesites if his remains were scattered over a dozen or so square meters—I could not say exactly to what degree this policy is pursued: a knuckle? A metacarpal?—as long as the remains are of known origin. And if a bone should turn out to be French or German, to each his own: it is transferred over to its rightful nation of origin.

On the French side, remains were automatically put into ossuaries. If identification has occurred (nearly a miracle, given the few resources dedicated to this task) the family is advised and inquiries are made as to whether they wish to recover the remains for a private funeral. Naturally, in the vast majority of cases, the answer is in the negative—what does one do with the bones of a great-grandfather?—and the remains are gathered into the nearest available ossuary. On the German side, the route to the ossuary is immediate, without detours. As for me, if someone were to ask my opinion, we should touch nothing and leave the remains exactly where they are, protected in their own world, in their time-patinated shroud of earth.

In fact, that is in large part what the British did. As early as 1917 it was decided that, wherever possible, bodies would be left where they had been buried by their comrades in arms and families were not permitted to repatriate the remains of their loved ones. This decision is the reason for the constellation of British military cemeteries that dot the Western Front and the entirety of the battlefields where British and Dominion troops fought. It is only since the Falklands/Malvinas War that Great Britain repatriates her dead.

The largest cemeteries are near field hospitals. One can therefore imagine that the smaller the cemetery, the deeper the bond between the gravedigger and the soldier he buried there: a friend, a neighbor, a parent. That is exactly what happened at Railway Hollow Cemetery. There, the graves for the "Accrington Pals," the boys from the small town of Accrington who had signed up together and died together around Serre and Hétebunne on July 1st 1916, were dug by their surviving Pals. In such cemeteries there is no rank or social class, no religion or ethnic origin. There is only the immensity of grief; the war.

***

As of this morning I have a new means of locomotion: an electric wheelchair that, strictly speaking, is more electric golf cart than chair and that will afford me greater mobility with less pain. This innovation in my life is the result of a long and complicated process of deliberation. First, I had to admit to myself that I had lost a great deal of autonomy and that walking had become problematic; next, I had to concede that it was increasingly difficult for me to stand upright for any length of time; and, finally, that crisscrossing the museum without assistance had now become impossible. There are forty-five steps from the entrance of the museum to the Welcome Desk; then fifteen steps from Welcome to the elevator that takes me up to my office, and another fifteen from the elevator to my office on the garden level. From office to Welcome Desk, one hundred yards, round trip, a mere one hundred paces for someone with legs as long as mine. A hundred yards is a frightfully long way; a hundred yards of repressed grimacing and muffled sighing.

My doctors were against my availing myself of such a machine: To give in to this easy solution, they said, would weaken my ability to walk on my own without any assistance, lessen my locomotion radius. "Well," one doctor finally conceded, "I don't live inside your skin, I don't walk in your shoes. . . ." thus summing up the situation exactly. Indeed, they cannot live inside my skin, or walk in my shoes. And, on a good day, my *locomotion radius* is a few hundred yards with several pauses. Is that what they mean by autonomy? I try to walk as much as is possible, to exercise those rebellious muscles of mine who exact a toll for every effort, even the simple act of standing upright.

My four-wheeler has no cause to be jealous of those tricycles lined up at the museum entrance wall: I don't have to do anything; no effort on my part is required in order to go forward. All I have to do is press a switch on the knob of my handlebars in order for my chariot to advance smoothly at a speed of my choosing. I have thus left the world of abled for that of the dis-abled: the sticker on the inside of my windshield no longer lies: the Director of the Historial is indeed handicapped.

I already know which people will avert their eyes, which will clumsily come up to me and quiz me as if I had to justify myself to them: "What's this? You are ill?" And I can predict those—fewer in number—who will change absolutely nothing in their demeanor towards me and will continue to include me as a fellow member of the same human race. They will ask about my health exactly as they always have and, on the off chance I ask for their help, they will lend it to me with neither ostentation nor superiority.

I did not choose to work at the Historial because I was sick. I wanted to switch the rhythm of my life for different reasons, one of which was a growing weariness. I attributed those aches to stress and to the intensity of my working hours; and to age, as I was approaching forty. . . . Now that I have passed that mark, I feel like an old man. My life is no less intense, but the stress is of a different sort: I manage it to suit me because it is only the result of projects I myself initiate—a positive and controllable stress. As I have a high opinion of the job I do and of the role I need to play, I have not sought to work less; I merely work differently. I am mindful of my body and my strength; I curtail movement.

The people around me are remarkable. They all conspire to reduce any physical effort on my part to the strict minimum necessary; chairs are silently and anonymously vacated for me, and I am spared any pity or commiseration-filled gawking. The only thing I experience is sincere empathy. That, in fact, is also what the Historial stands for: Every day, the museum welcomes hundreds of visitors; one of them will talk to you about the death of a grandfather; another about how the brotherhood of ancestors came to be decimated; yet another will show you letters from a great-uncle to a great-aunt; and, because she has no way of doing so herself, one will come to entrust you with the safekeeping of precious mementos. She knows that, here at the Historial, they will live on and survive her; that making this gift is a way to attain a piece of immortality through her name on a plaque and on the index of the museum's inventory. If you do not possess a deeply rooted compassion at the core of your character, you will not long suffer what some harsh observers call "that constant bellyaching." As for me, I am never called upon to invoke that quality from deep within: I stay in my office and meet only those people with whom my secretary has made an appointment after asking me whether I wish to meet with them. Thus, while I profess that I place what is truly human at the center of all things, I am rarely if ever challenged to test that credo in the light of real-world fact. I wish to give full credit to those who, with a smile or an expression, make my days less dreary and give me the desire to experience tomorrow. Indeed, let me give thanks to all who surround me and those who—on a daily basis—turn the Historial into a place entirely out of the ordinary.

As for my soldiers, my deepest admiration goes to them. This is neither idolization nor the manifestation of a morbid streak: To where would my previous life—the one without them, the race of ambition-filled rats in which I exhausted myself hopping from one train to the next—have led? To more money? More recognition? I would not be the person I am today if I were anywhere other than at the Historial. This platitude is an absolute truth. Without the cemeteries, the monuments, the commemorations, the museum and its staff, the memorabilia, the history and the historians, I would have plunged into grief, I would be a lump of bitterness and regrets— but you should not infer from the curt tone of my words any dark tendencies, any acceptance of death, or the sad surrender of a cripple seeking identification with other cripples by sitting on their graves. No, that is not what this is about; this is about images that cling to your body, stories that touch your heart; it is about glances exchanged across the span of a century. I do not seek to compare that which is not comparable: I have been taught to manage my pain, a pharmacist stands at the ready to offer me a cornucopia of all the analgesics I need (even if they don't completely eradicate all pain), not one of my anxiety spells is stronger than my anxiety medication, once a month a psychotherapist listens to me for an hour talk about my physical and psychological pains, I live with the woman I love, and the moment I call out my children's names, they answer my call.

Nor is this about invalidating my feelings by condemning myself to silence presumably with the justification that those whom I observe across the past century have suffered more, that the mud through which these men trod was wetter and colder than the tiles on which my *Homo occidentalis* slippers tread today. It is true the names on the grave markers at the Australian Memorial at Villiers-Bretonneux or on the crosses at the military cemetery of Cléry-Sur-Somme are unfamiliar to me; but they are as unfamiliar as would be a twin of mine, separated at birth and about whom I knew nothing, but about whom my heart would know all. Even though from time to time I feel the need to get some distance, to come up for air for a while, to unfetter my heart from such romantic imaginings, I nonetheless always return to them: I mourn these men, I watch over them, my brothers from that other world. I care for the cowards, the traitors, the murderers and the heroes and the saints and the Flaubert, Schiele or Dickens who would never come to be. They were all young boys once; they loved and were loved; they all had a last name or a first name or a nickname they did not like or want. They all went through the meat-grinder of total war, the kind that tears the youngest away from the family, or the strongest, or the most handsome, only to throw him away into the clangor of steel that shreds into shards and shrapnel. Those who come back are returned older, weaker, uglier. Indeed, no one has ever—ever—won a war.

For each mutilated face, how many broken souls whose suffering is invisible? For each missing arm, how many imperceptible scars? There was the case of this man who, having passed the age of ninety, invariably spent Sundays plucking tiny fragments of shrapnel that the flesh in his arms continued to expel all these decades after being wounded by artillery fire at Verdun. There was another man who slept only in a seated position because his gassed lungs were too feeble to lift the weight of his rib cage. And what of the tens of millions of nights spoiled by nightmare? And the millions of smiles now extinct? What of all those about whom the history books say nothing, whose private stories are merely reflections of silence or of peculiar obsessions, the visible part of icebergs of horror and agony. They were never heard, they did not speak up because they thought themselves the lucky ones, the ones whose pain was lesser than that of their disfigured companions in arms. Nowadays, we pay attention and treat post-traumatic shock; psychological pain is no longer grist for jokes. How long has this been so? Thirty years, forty, perhaps? Those men, they were part of another era—They were men who did not cry, did not complain, did not show their ailment, not even when drunk, not even among friends. If they talked, they talked about their feats, "their" war; but they never talked about that other war, the private one, the one that kept them awake at night. What I am writing about here, they have all kept buried deep in their hearts: That does not lessen the sting of the burn.

Whoever sees me without knowing the nature of my affliction cannot grasp the extent of that affliction. I limp, I grimace; but nothing else is perceptible. A careful observer, however, might notice that I repeatedly change hands on the spoon just to stir my coffee; that I ceaselessly squirm in my chair; that I drive a car with gloves on; in other words, that

25

any position or sensation of touch is bearable only for a very short period of time.

I am fully aware that this is what illness is; "being ill" proceeds from a range of manifestations and symptoms that are just as psychological as they are physical. I lean to neither one side nor the other, but accept both: They go together, that much is undeniable. *To be* is essentially to be on a stage, in an appearance before others and yourself; to "*be ill*" is no exception to this rule. If I lift my hand, I proclaim my courage; if I lower it, I admit my despair; creased eyebrows—an indication of pain; bags under my eyes—a great deal of pain.

Illness excuses all my faults and exaggerates my virtues. I am "strong," "courageous," "modest;" my cynicism becomes "lucid thinking" and "a dispassionate distancing." Nevertheless, I estrange myself from others and they from me. I am apart, in a world with blurred borders, where Terrae Incognitae drift, where darkness leaves its indelible mark even in broad daylight. When I receive a visitor in my office, I am the Director. When I escort the visitor out to the door, I am that handicapped person. When I speak at a conference, I am the Director; but when I walk to my seat I am once again that handicapped person. I must ascertain each destination in terms of motion, elevation, comfort of seating and, once I sit down, where my cane will fit. People around me do likewise on my behalf: They study floor plans and train schedules. They tell me I look tired when I feel fit and that I look fit when I feel tired. As for me, the pain is constant but I think about it only when I listen to my body's complaints; I have learned how to be free of the pain—as long as it is not intolerable—but she is a truly faithful companion who knows how to make herself heard and respected.

My body and I have never really been on very intimate terms. This odd shell full of tubes that makes unseemly noises, that stinks the minute you forget to maintain it, and that you have to feed at least once a day lest you spend your waking hours worrying about the stomach's empty growls is—at its best—useful; but it takes thirty years to master all of its intricate functions and, by then, they have all started their decline. My height is just another source of discomfort: my shirt sleeves are always too short, my jackets all have to be tailor-made, my trousers are always without cuffs, and I already know the purchase of my coffin will incur a surcharge: "He was so tall, you see. . . ." I scare those who bump into me in a hallway or on a street corner; I intimidate small children and I am the first to notice incipient bald spots. I have been "outside the norm" for so long, I no longer really pay attention and I could not tell you who is six feet tall and who is five foot six; whatever the case, to me, every person is a short person.

As a result of having to behave like an old man for an increasingly larger part of my daily activities, I am unable to distinguish what is due to being forty and what is due to illness. It is only through doctors' comments that I am able to ascertain that a particular ache is due to "normal" aging. *A contrario* I must stand straight, suck in my gut and hold my head high in order to fight off the cascading effects of assuming positions that are comfortable but ill-suited to my body. Already, my feet require corrective action; soon it will be my knees. I sense that I am about to enter a forest of complications in which, inevitably, I will get lost. I am fragmented: I live in a body that, with each passing day, belongs to me less and less; a body whose multiple parts one after the other declare their independence. That is how I discover connections between body parts or organs I did not even know existed, but who make themselves known to me through successive acts of rebellion.

Fatigue overwhelms my days. I wake up tired, I go to bed tired and to sleep is exhausting. Any prolonged contact of one part of my body with any other is excruciating and when I shift positions at night, I do so gingerly, careful to avoid sudden movement. From time to time, in spite of all these precautions, some effort will exact a howl of pain: She is always there, my jealous companion, even in the deepest recesses of my nights.

I hear myself answering "yes" without even having thought about the question "Are you feeling alright?" Could I even think of answering otherwise? If I were to answer "no" to all the people who ask me this question, my mornings would boil down to endless repetitions of pitying stares or sullen pouts. No one likes to see pain. In others, we seek to keep it at a safe distance and—if you must talk about it—you have no idea what to say; you are embarrassed. I don't like talking about my pain: It always sounds like I am complaining. And yet I should, from time to time, come to terms with it, to release the pressure built up by the unsaid, the unspoken, the stifled hardships, the powerlessness, the anger. The words "it hurts" have become difficult for me to say. I no longer say them.

As far as I am able, I try not to compound psychological pain on top of the physical. Day follows day, each similar yet parsed differently by the rhythms of changeable weather: rain, snow, thunder, blue sky, rain, rain, rain, mist. The sun would be my best friend, were it not for the fact that he reminds me of my inability to enjoy a gorgeous summer's day: there will be no hike, no day at the beach, no picnic in the forest.

The mind wants to master the body—even if the body is certain to exact its revenge. This kind of stupid battle quickly leads you into the antechamber of madness. The self fragments itself, becomes two, three then four or five entities: the mind, the torso, the hands, the intestines, the diaphragm . . . You become afraid; you moan, you pat yourself, you sweat; your breathing shallows. You must gather up all the disparate parts of yourself, all the while acknowledging that pain will take many forms and that she is you just as much as hunger, desire, smell and touch, fear and angst are you. In addition, you must learn that there is an unknown, private—no, secret—part of you, that will know how to make you listen to its complaint even if you do not understand why it is complaining. I need to repel all of these attacks of the body against itself, this guerrilla warfare in which no side can win. To paraphrase Joffre, "I am eroding myself." Yes, I am chipping away at myself in the battle of me against me. I have become the battlefield—the battlefield of an unwinnable war.

I imagine the handicapped life that awaits me, and I prepare for it. We have all heard about the "Social Security Gap," a constant in France's political debates of the last fifteen years. Given that he has become the last link, the "gatekeeper," in a long chain of mechanisms that begins with the Minister of Finance and ends with you, your "Primary Care Physician" has a mandate to firmly apply the brakes on costs. I venture to guess that every PCP is evaluated on his or her ability to apply a tourniquet to the local share of the national hemorrhage that robs the Social Security Administration of the ability to perform its socio-medical mission. Needless to say, his evaluation of you—before he even looks at your chart—is most likely not very positive. You know it, and he knows you know it. The trick will be to get him to admit that the symptoms you describe are so obviously real and plain to see that they can't possibly be faked; as my grandfather used to say, "we're not out of the woods yet."

I consider myself an intelligent person, and I place great faith in those people who share this opinion with me—which, of course, further reinforces the opinion I have of myself; but am I intelligent enough to make the Social Security Primary Care Physician understand that I am not faking my pain and that, no, I cannot move in that way without howling and, again no, I am not pretending to howl. When I wrote that I imagine a handicapped life, I should have said, rather, that I think about it: imagining has dream-like connotations; being forced to leave the Historial is far more akin to a nightmare.

***

Within a twenty-mile radius of Péronne, every significant intersection has a signpost pointing to the "Historial of the Great War." When I have become an invalid, and am no longer at the Historial, I won't be able to travel even a few miles before one of those signposts reminds me of what I once was, and what I have become. In that limbo will be the me of today who contemplates images from this devastating future, the me who sees this possibility as increasingly probable with every passing day, who notices that the car is more difficult to drive, that the right leg rebels when asked to press on the gas pedal, that it is fortunate an automatic transmission obviates the need for a clutch under the left foot, that I need to start thinking about retrofitting hand-operated accelerator and brake controls, that I have become the tiny hazelnut in the jaws of a monstrous nutcracker that bites down on me and mashes me, and that I am so afraid of agony that I shudder from fright at the thought of pain.

Will I be able to accept my own decay? I will be nothing; or, at best, the former Director of the Historial: Yes, he's the one who left because . . . But what else will I be? A good father? A good husband? Will that be all there is to me? What will I do to feel useful, needed? How will I fill my days? Shall I start drinking, or put an end to my life? Is there nothing but despair ahead? Will illness ultimately turn me into a wooden-voiced puppet, motionless from fear of pain at the slightest movement? How vain I was to once have believed I had a Destiny. The thought of death no longer frightens me; instead, it makes me bitter: what purpose does this all serve? I will have passed on my genes, nothing more. I will have given life to human beings who, in turn, reproduce and perhaps one day there will be, amid the flood of my descendants, a shining nugget—unless of course it is a butcher or a dictator. Or perhaps I will have perpetuated a long lineage in continuation of the one from which I come: somewhere between *Australopithecus* and *Homo habilisimus.*

30

Whatever the case, I will not exist, I will no longer exist, and my egocentric ways will have been of interest to no one; my existence in vain and my sole function on this earth having been to produce and ejaculate two spermatozoa that shared in the making of my two children. I can howl, I can write, hoping I will be read—admired, perhaps—but better yet understood. I can put on the mask of a wounded man, but I need only stretch out my arm to pick up a phone and speak to my wife, my children, my friends. And even if it leaves no trace of itself other than another line item in a phone bill, even if tomorrow or a month from now I have completely forgotten the reason I even made the call, I need only have stretched out my arm to say "I love you, I miss you. See you tonight." I am nothing more than a selfish marionette that exists only for those by whom he is loved and who, no matter what he might think, and whatever his life may look like to him, nonetheless has his life still ahead of him. True, it is a life about which I know nothing, one whose length and quality and tenure is unknown; one which might yet create as much surprise as pain, as much beauty as filth; a life to be composed, to be cherished and from which to give back at least as much as was received. Indeed, yes, every time I drive my car, there will be a sign telling me how to get back to the Historial, and there will be a cemetery whose steles and crosses will remind me of who I am and where and when I live; of how stupid certain obsessions are, and of how fortunate I am to live in a free and democratic country. That is what I must keep saying, that I what I must keep thinking. I need to stop contemplating that gaping chasm that is spreading, over there, beneath the plaque that bears my surname, name and date of birth engraved above the blank space reserved for the as-yet-unknown date of the day I die.

***

On Sundays, weather permitting, we go to our pond. It one of those thousands of ponds created by Picardy's rivers, from the Somme to the Avre, the Cologne to the Bresle. We rent the pond with our friends Kiki and René. René is one of those people who understands without needing to have things explained to him. Kiki—her Greek name Vasiliki became "Kiki" for short—can let you know, with a mere glance or the touch of her hand, that she loves you and worries about you.

When we go to the pond, we fish. The children are silent, absorbed in the stillness of their fishing poles. Lounging on lawn chairs, the wives read. There is a rustle of the wind as it flows through the birches, and a croak of frogs; René and I do not speak. And if the wind were to ripple the surface of our pond, or our fishing corks begin to bob, and we happen to snag a pike or a roach, we limit the conversation to practical exchanges of information. At the pond, there are no discussions, no debates: we let time flow by and we savor it, whether it's raining or scorching hot; we let the seconds tick by and we stop thinking. There, you feel closer to yourself, apart from others, almost real, almost true. We do not go there to fill our baskets with fish. In fact, we practice catch and release. There is only the pleasure of being there; of being near one another in a world where sound is born out of silence.

I have a special spot which René created just for me: There is a chair and a pole-holder under the canopy of birch branches. We fish on the fly: no reel, no line to pull in; just a pole, a bob, and a hook. Even if I have difficulty threading the bait onto the hook, I don't let it show. I don't want to be spoiled to the point that I will let someone else bait my line. The same goes for pulling the hook out of a pike's mouth: I do not curse nor even mutter; I merely apply myself. And everyone (except perhaps the pike) pretends there is no problem, just as we all pretend that my hands shake because I am cold, that my movements are abrupt because I am anxious and that I have difficulty speaking because the rosé is just so darn good.

From the car to the pond: one hundred yards. Before he suggested we become co-renters of this pond, René had studied the pathway, imagining what obstacles I might encounter at every turn. He made certain no branch could block my way, he even projected the growth of the hazelnut trees and how we might have to prune them; he examined every foot of the trail in order to foresee any pitfalls. Naturally, he said nothing of this to me; but from the very first visit I sensed his careful attention to detail. I became aware of his concern when my feet caught once or twice on a root. I know he wasn't worried about having failed, but rather that he fervently hoped he had found just the right pond that would give our two families an opportunity to be together without it becoming either complicated or painful for me.

From my house to the pond, it takes forty minutes by car. We cross the full breadth of the Santerre Plain. It is inordinately flat, incredibly green and immeasurably boring for those who do not know how to look: the extraordinary flatness is punctuated by bumps and barely seen crevices, with apparently flat stretches that are really inclines steep enough to rob a fit cyclist of his leg power; and for the driver, there are unexpected curves that arise out of nowhere in front of you after miles and miles of a straight road.

When observed from a warrior's perspective, however, the plain is altogether something else. This broad, flat plain has without a doubt long been the joy of many a cavalry officer, whether his steed was of flesh or steel: The absence of any salient features indeed lends itself to the charge, with sword or bayonet. And yet, if you were to get down to ground level, to lie down on the ground or perhaps even bury yourself underground, you would soon recognize that small embankment for the sizable hill that it really is; that this hillock is a crest and that these seemingly flat one hundred yards of terrain are more strenuous than the cruelest of marathons—if indeed a marathon were to be run under a hail of lead.

By 1914, the pathetically naive images of sword or bayonet charges of wars past, of the gleam of uniforms under azure skies, were shredded by artillery and machine-gun fire; what few fantasies the military still harbored were shattered. So, we dug in; we dug holes in which to be protected; we linked our hole to our neighbor's hole and created a trench. But that didn't stop the killing; in fact we put more effort into killing, inventing new and better weapons with which to fight from one trench to the other. We dug in deeper. We built and hardened bunkers, erected forts. We killed in massive numbers, thousands of dead every day, thousands of death notices being delivered to families; and, sometimes, even the town mayor himself wore black. You'd be on the lookout for him, you'd tremble and pray please god let him pass my door, let so-and-so be well, because we've been good Christians and this just can't be; and we harvest the fields or assemble the bombs because Victory is still the best way for Pierre, Jean or Emile to return soon; so don't even come near my door, Monsieur le Maire[3]; and, because we are good citizens of France, because we've been attentive to the teachings of the Republic, and because we've all read *Two Children on a Tour of France*, we all know where our duty lies; so, if need be, we'll bow down our heads to hide the tears, we'll wear black and hold high in front of our faces our veils moistened by sorrow.

The Battle of the Somme began with an artillery barrage that lasted five days and five nights without ever letting up. July 1st 1916, on a front line twenty-five miles long, the actual offensive began. British forces bore most of the burden, as the French were quite busy indeed at Verdun. The campaign lasted until mid-November of that year. Those six months of combat were horrific: 420,000 British killed (80,000 of whom

---

3   In the smaller towns, the Mayor would go in person to notify the next of kin of a soldier's death.

were never found); on the French side, 200,000 dead (of whom 27,000 are still missing). As for the Germans, they lost 437,000 men on those fields. That brings the total number of killed or presumed dead to close to one million men. Some historians insist the true number is probably closer to 1.2 million. If you think of the battlefield as roughly 200 square miles—25 miles long by 8 miles wide—it means one dead every fifty feet. While this absurd calculation applies only to the Battle of the Somme, you need to keep in mind that from 1915 through November 1918, combat never ceased. Such is what I call the equation of horror; an equation that has no real solution.

My universe is minuscule, constricted within the borders of my house, the museum and the city of Péronne. Even so, I need only walk a hundred steps from my office and the entire world reveals itself to me: American posters, British knickknacks, Soviet commemorative plates with cubist motifs, German soldiers' beer steins. . . . If I walk another hundred steps, I have all the continents at my fingertips: uniforms from Indochina, hats from Australia, knives from China; and over there Canada, South Africa, Senegal and Cote d'Ivoire. Four miles out, there is the cemetery of La Chapelette with its Nepalese and Indian tombs; at six miles out, the Villiers-Carbonnel Cemetery of French colonial troops from French West Africa and French Equatorial Africa; eight miles out is the Tincourt New British Cemetery and the Chinese, Italian, Sikh and Gurka battalions; fifteen miles away is Longueval, the South African Memorial Museum and replica of the Fort du Cap; and, finally, at 35 miles from the Historial, the statue of a caribou howling at the moon commemorates the brave volunteers from Newfoundland. . . . How many are they, my fellow humans scattered here and there, who sleep unnoticed and unknown beneath my feet? The entire world is resting in our French fields, our forests, and by the side of our roads. A Vietnamese proximal phalanx, an Australian metacarpal, a Chinese cemetery, Canadian and South African skulls, a femur from Senegal and a tibia from Cote d'Ivoire . . . Such thoughts neither haunt nor obsess me; but they do return from time to time, even though I belong to the world of the living and even though I let the dead rest in peace where they lie. The thoughts come and go, but they pass. In the fields of the Somme, the wheat that for nearly a century has made the bread for the living has been sprouting atop human remains. The fertile plains of my living world are really buried battlefields known only to roots, rabbits, gophers and worms.

At eye level, the Somme is a vast plain but, at the bottom of a trench, the Somme stinks, and below the verdant surface of the Santerre Plateau lie tens of thousands of corpses. Insidious at first, this thought insinuated itself into my psyche and has now become part of the ordinary strangeness of daily life. The Historial praises neither heroism nor self-sacrifice; nor does it exalt love of country or the quest for glory; rather, it celebrates the human being, the breadth of his suffering and the unfathomable depth of his stupidity. That is what I think about, Sundays by the pond.

War is all around me; at the museum, in my office, in the back rooms, in the gift shop, in the cafeteria. War, war, war; in Péronne, in the Somme Valley, in town, at home, the war is everywhere, but I am not inured to the faces of the wounded or the blank stares of the survivors; they are here, all around me as well. Every question, from visitors or friends, loved ones or compatriots, always brings me back to the war; and before my eyes, the double-amputees and torso-men with broken faces, faces without noses or lower jaws, they all dance. The war is terrifying and yet is part of my daily routine. I have no explanation for the fact that this causes me no pain; in fact, I feel an uncomfortable pride in being everything they can longer be, in being—in a word—a survivor. What an odd and arrogant thought.

In the areas where combat was the most fierce, there fell over a ton of explosives for every square yard. Of this ton, thirty percent failed to detonate. In order to dispose of this thirty percent, Civil Defense has to plan for seven centuries of explosives removal. Seven hundred years in which to fear and worry. On the site of the battle of Crécy, one no longer finds arrowheads. Bouvines[4] and Marignan[5] are now quaint towns. In the year 2650, in thirty generations, we will still be telling the youths of Picardy to beware of rusted metal, and the children of Verdun will know that it is dangerous to re-enact the Great War in the forests of Douaumont and that, in any case, it is in poor taste to do so.

When I want to convey a striking image or shake up the blank and blasé stares, that is the story I tell, the list I check off: one Frenchman in twenty-seven, ten million soldiers, a ton of explosives, thirty percent. In five hundred years, my generation will have been lumped and blended together with a truncated 20th century that began on August 1st, 1914 and no doubt ended in 1989 with the fall of the Berlin Wall. People will tally up the ten million of the First World War with the fifty million of the Second and will ask themselves what kind of barbarians we were to tolerate such a meaningless waste of human life. At the least, that is what I can hope for the citizens of 2510. For them, they who will be looking backward five hundred years, my generation will seem contemporary to that of the soldiers of the Somme.

***

---

4   The Battle of Bouvines took place on 27 July 1214, and ended the twelve-year Angevin-Flanders War.
5   1515 battle near the town of Marignano during the Italian Wars (Translator's notes)

Over time, you become accustomed to having someone at your side; someone about whom you think you know everything there is to know: the shape of the face, the curves of the body, the tiny imperfections, the obsessions, the pettiness and nobility of spirit; someone whose mannerisms, leitmotifs and limitations annoy you. But what happens when all of that disappears? Even when you are away only a few days, time passes more slowly, you remember the face, the curves, the mannerisms, the refrains and limitations. . . . And now you miss them all. You swear to yourself that, this time, when you get back, you will be patient and understanding, that you will love exactly as you did in those early days, that you will change everything; and then you return and a trifle bothers you, and then other trifles, and you end up repeating the same old gestures or absence of gestures, the same words and the same silences.

At all the intersections, in all the stairwells, under all the balconies—*She* waits for us; she is pleased when we puff on our cigarettes, she urges us to have a second serving of fries, she applauds when we overindulge. In the end, she takes everything; and if you are the first to leave with her, it does not matter, and if you are left behind, alone, you cry for those "trifles" that you once again miss: that face, that body, those leitmotifs. And she will flaunt her powers of persuasion in your face: She will boast that she has taken one infantryman out of three, one Frenchman out of twenty-seven: ten million men in four years.

When I hurt, when my bones and muscles ache, that is what I think about. It does not comfort me, nor does it make anything the least bit relative to anything else; but it does help me to become patient and loving, to listen to my children, to stand on my own feet and pay attention to those whom I love and appreciate. To know that ten million soldiers died between 1914 and 1918 changes nothing in the life I lead—except that my life is the sweeter for it. It is not that I owe these ten million dead anything but that, when I communicate my pain, I feel an obligation to maintain some kind of dignity or modesty.

My own story, my family history, also imposes sobriety and a modicum of silence. In 1914, my maternal great-grandfather left then German-occupied Lorraine to fight for the motherland of his heart, the French Republic. He was forty-two years old with eight children and earned a good living as a master woodworker. Assigned to what was then called "The Territorial," a division comprised of rear-echelon soldiers, the war should have been relatively quiet for him; but the scale of losses in front-line troops turned "The Territorial" into a combat division. He survived combat, but not the Spanish Flu of 1918. It took his widow more than ten years to collect on his soldier's pension: Her husband had had the bad judgment in his younger days to let himself be forcibly conscripted into the Kaiser's army. Since he was born in occupied Lorraine, he was, technically, German. His son, my grandfather, had very blurred memories of his seven brothers and sisters, his only clear childhood images being those of a child who has known hunger.

On my father's side, we were bankers. This great-grandfather was also forty-something at the onset of the war. but he fought the war in a very different way, keeping his body and his assets well protected. I am not ashamed of it, nor am I proud. Death takes on many forms: death of the body, death of conscience, death of the soul.

Given all of that, yes, I feel I must show some kind of dignity, some form of restraint. I want to be perceived as a decent sort of person. I ascribe no particular moral value to this desire; it is neither homage nor tribute to anything. Given the circumstances of my life and the social position I hold, it seems logical to me that I should feel this way. I do not know whether in different circumstances I might behave differently; but I would like to think not.

***

You needn't have been a military genius to realize that any attempt at a breakthrough in a landscape such as this one would inevitably be doomed to failure. The inevitable occurred: The Chemin des Dames offensive was a disaster. In two months' time there were 400,000 French and German dead. How could anyone have believed it would be possible to storm that hillock peppered with machine-gun nests and fortified caves? It seems that two years of static trench warfare had not taught the French high command the folly of such ambitions: They had not yet learned breakthroughs were no longer possible and victory could not be won at the point of a bayonet. The era of heroic charges had passed, and one had to be far removed indeed from the front lines not to have noticed. They still believed a soldier's readiness to fight trumped technology and that machine-gun nests could not long resist the courage and determination of our seasoned troops. Failure, therefore, had to be a sign of cowardice and betrayal—both of which could absolutely not be tolerated. There were executions, the rhetoric was ratcheted up; but they had to backpedal very quickly, or else the entire army would have been embarrassed.

Weary. They must have been weary, or discouraged, or fatalistic. You are afraid; you are alone; you are just a man and you don't cry. Yes, you'll go over the top once more; you'll rush the enemy line ahead as you pray that the bursts of lead and steel might knock you down and produce one of those beautiful wounds, the one that sends you home not quite whole, but whole enough, or at least alive. And if you make it to the enemy line, please Lord, let me not have to slash and stab or disembowel, kill. Please, Lord, let them all be dead by the time I get there. Please, Lord, let's be done with this; kill them all.

The ones we left behind, will they be the same ones we come home to? Will we still have any appetite for love once our souls explode with horrific memories? And they who made the shell-casings or plowed the fields while we were gone, will they still have any use for half a man? And the children, who wonder about the dark circles under our eyes, will they really understand the meaning of the name "Verdun;" will they know Chaulnes or Thiepval? Is there even a future for us, we who will be coming home?

My hands are pale and silky; their fingers glide along my piano keyboard, imperceptibly less deftly than they did yesterday. My legs have trouble holding up this torso and its distended stomach; but everything above the diaphragm still belongs to me and obeys me, for the moment. If one day this part also escapes my control, I will have had fair warning; there will be no surprises—a few bitter regrets, perhaps—as I slowly suffocate.

I would like to be able to write that there are moments of happiness. Yes, there are some moments: they are simple and pure, and they cast such an intense light that, within the gloom that surrounds me, I am blinded. The warmth of these moments comforts me like a salve on my chest. For too long, I searched for an absolute happiness, one that would come to me and never leave me and that would feed itself in the inexhaustible depths of a sublime and perfect me, at last measuring up to the heights of my expectations. In seeking too much, I exhausted myself, and illness easily struck me down when I was weak: I was barely recovering from a profound disappointment that had left me with a feeling of loss amid a vast and barren wasteland. At the age of thirty-five I was finally leaving adolescence behind me. It was in these early days of adulthood that I had to confront another "me," one about whom I knew nothing and whose strengths and weaknesses I entirely misjudged. Today, there is nothing to conquer, nothing to remove, no malfunctioning part to replace or no amputation of which might cure "the rest." There is only my mind, which does not understand the assault my body is perpetrating upon itself: A mind that searches for obvious remedies, which, no doubt, do not exist. Thus, the moments of happiness end up being obscured by a single question which requires no answer, because there is none: why?

I have discovered a body that no longer keeps me upright but which, when it carried me effortlessly, I used to disdain. How many times did I use to run without even being aware I was running? And when, in an effort to go faster, my legs and arms were cycling rhythmically through their contracting and stretching phases, how many times did my heart start racing excitedly without my even asking it to do so? Why didn't I at the time relish the ability of the different parts of my body to work in such harmony, synchronizing the rhythm of my breath to the movement of legs and arms? And if I happened to experience the next day the aches of muscle exertion, I experienced them with a smile, as I poked fun at myself for these spasms which were, in the end, nothing more than the fair price to pay for an exhilarating earlier effort. Yes, I laughed at my cramps; but measured against the yardstick of my tears today, the bursts of laughter of those days are very small-scale indeed.

Today, I dream of being someone else, of abandoning these trappings of the once lanky poseur now beaten down by life: I dream about being able to run again, to stroll wherever I please, to go on long outings, play a sport, ride horses or go swimming. I dream about waking up feeling rested, about feeling content as I open the shutters, about smiling at my children, smiling at the one I love. It is much too late for regrets; it is only through my suffering that I have been able to measure the value of what I have lost. I must cry now because I regret not having laughed when the time was ripe for laughter. You at the bottom of the pit, at the back of the bar, in the arms of that one-night-stand Marie, haven't you been sorry that you didn't laugh when it was time for laughter? And how many more have cried for not having laughed with you? Yes, your youth was wild and the war took it all, the laughter and the tears all jumbled together. In the arrhythmia of my limp, I lead the parade of an army of ghosts. Come to think of it, I do have moments of happiness; they come to me in the tempest of my mood swings and in the low grumble of my pains.

Yesterday, the pain was so fierce that I had to leave the Historial and have someone bring me home. I had to abandon my post. Giant pincers clawed at my ankles, my knees, my wrists, elbows and shoulders; their steel jaws tightened around my crunching cartilage and bone while thin, long needles pierced my leg and arm muscles through and through. I was, for three hours, a stranger to myself, outside my own skin, trying to hold this howling body at a distance from me.

Was this the first of many attacks that will inescapably lead to complete disability? Until now, I had thought the change would be sudden, that there would be a "last day" on which I could leave the Historial and my working life with a sense of a task accomplished. Now, I am no longer certain. The romantic notion of the wounded leader guiding his troops with the very last measure of his strength has given way to the vision of a man trying to do whatever he can to keep on living decently and with the respect of others and himself. Was it improper to thus stop temporarily because the pain was too intense? The answer is not altogether clear. I have, fighting each other within me, the Byronic hero and the man in pain; each takes up too much space inside my own skin, and the fury of their quarrel amplifies the waves of anxiety that submerge me at night. Working occupies the mind, but saps the body. By working, I exhaust myself; by sleeping, I erode myself from the inside. Nothing good can possibly come from such ambivalence.

The objects that surround me and the shadows that encircle me all whisper this: *Decency requires that you persevere, upright, in the silence of your pain; that you spare your loved ones too much moodiness, too much despair.* My cane still keeps me standing; I limp, but I go forward and tomorrow is not necessarily a risky assumption. I remember the gaze of that soldier who carried his unconscious comrade on his back: the eyes of a man filled with terror as well as determination. He is returning from a charge with the few others who survived, and he has discovered on this July 1st, 1916 that nothing in his life from now on will ever be identical to what he has known; that, at this precise moment, this moment when he lifts his eyes towards the lens of the camera filming him, he is being catapulted into an "after" about which he will never be able to speak because he has encountered that which cannot be said in words; he has crossed into that territory where emotions are storms of devastation and where not a single word can justify its own utterance. The tepid blood that drips down his back is the only reminder that he is still of this world, a survivor, a "more alive," who now must occupy a special place amidst and yet far from the rest of us common mortals. He is not broken; he has his arms, his legs, and a face people will recognize; he is whole and yet entirely and forever apart from the rest of us. And so, it is then I stop talking: I reflect on all those who will be submerged elsewhere, further away, in the nauseating rhythm of the ceaseless tides of war.

Pictures, films, memorabilia and their histories, all the tiny stories, come to my rescue. The one of the man who reaps one-handed, of the one-legged country constable, the missing-parts-men. . . . I feel their stories have never been heard because they never said a word. Parades of these veterans always exacted silence from the crowd, because the veterans were all silent (except perhaps for a few extremists of February 6th, 1934).[6] All they ever hoped for was peace; but the very desire to protect the Nation from any further

6   On that day, some veterans joined massive street protests in Paris. The day is remembered—rightly or wrongly—as an attempted fascist coup d'état. (Translator's note)

insanity of war may very well be what led to war, again. Even today, in deference to our veterans of the Great War, we talk about "guaranteed employment," and signs in the subways and buses still remind us to reserve or give up our seats for the GIWs, the Great Invalids of War; many a schoolyard still echoes with the stories of Monsieur Gaston's broom and his flat leather mask which hides the unspeakable and unimaginable. And yet, they are all gone, those veterans have all died by now, and I say we did not ever hear them because they never once complained.

Like everyone, I am battered about by life. I get bruised; I stumble, get up and stumble again. There are some bruises you acquire and soon forget; there are the more serious injuries, which hurt at the time and when they scar and heal; and then there are the wounds that sweep you to another place, like a torrent of sorrow and hate that drowns the mind. You try to stop thinking, to stop suffering. You try Zen meditation or Buddhism, you learn relaxation techniques because you think you can tame the body by training the mind; you implore Christ or Mohammed, you give yourself unto God. As best you can, you move forward—sometimes standing up, sometimes lying down—rarely proud, but still alive; and you delay, minute by minute, the second of your last breath. You don't even think about it: Death is far off; it does not really exist. It might happen that someone close to you will pass and, just for a few days, you feel insignificant and fragile. Then, daily routine reclaims the upper hand, and the purr of our settled lives assuages our fears. Of course, I am afraid; but I cannot live if to live is to be in constant fear. I try to postpone my anxieties until at least tomorrow. Sometimes, I succeed; other times, not. But there is only one alternative to being alive and that alternative I have already rejected; it is not in the realm of my possibilities: I cannot kill myself.

"You never know," my assistant Séverine told me as she filed away a folder in a drawer, "in ten years you might be glad to discover we kept this file." In ten years' time? I won't be at the Historial in ten years. I am not certain I'll be here next year, let alone ten. In fact, I have begun to delegate many of my responsibilities. I invest less and less of myself in projects that are likely to have little or no impact on the future direction of the institution. I assign others to fulfill my duties of public relations, regionally and around the country. I am taking some distance in very measured steps, hopefully without anyone noticing. I have decided to plan my legacy while preparing to become incapacitated. The recent experience of having been forced to leave work and return home was too difficult for me to bear. I wish to depart in all good conscience, not merely to fade away after a series of crises that would ultimately force me to accept my status as an invalid. I feel as though I might be planning my own burial, with the odd corollary that I would be fulfilling that common fantasy of listening to the eulogies while attending my funeral. It is conceited, perhaps, but I want there to have been a before and an after to my time at this institution. I want to be able to leave the Historial surrounded by all those who made me love the place, helped me make it better—all those with whom I have worked and whose presence enriched my life.

I think about all there would be to do in order for me to fill my empty hours: go back to studying Latin and grammar, write, live with no stress other than the stress of having nothing that *must* be done—perhaps an opportunity to polish up my French classical education. I will of course have to force myself to do some physical exercise in order to push back the onset of complete palsy. No doubt, I will be mostly disabled or passive, but I do want to demonstrate everything that I am still capable of doing. I have a good many talents, I think, and I should be able to nurture them without regard for how much time that might take. The pen will carry me; it will probably strip me of all my masks, and make me rediscover the vastness of the unexpected worlds that sleep deep within me. I want to be the bridge between the two banks that the river of a century separates; and I want to do so without any complacency at either the insight afforded me by my condition or the advantages of my office. I am not trying to create an opus, or indeed even to "make literature." I merely seek to have existed in some way other than merely sitting behind a desk or lounging at home, crying over my lot in life.

To you, my children, I owe all of me. My beautiful Daphné, I want to hold out at least until your wedding. I want to see you dance in the arms of the one you will have chosen. I want to see the sparkle of love in your eyes. Will you be ashamed of your pot-bellied father who slouches in an easy chair from which he rarely rises? Will he never stand up, that paunchy dad? Yes, I will be there; I will hold on for you, to see you grow up and emerge from the awkward years into which you are now gleefully rushing. I want to see you be you; the you after the rejection of all pretense, the you who will have overcome the drama of childhood and the mistakes of adolescence. I want to see you for the beautiful person you are; I want to rejoice in your joy. I want to find out if you really do become a veterinarian; if your passion for Silkies, Ardenaise and Padua hens (silly me, who thought there was only one kind of chicken and one kind of hen!) is still as intense then as it is overwhelming today; if you finally inherit your father's lankiness; and if you will finally let me embrace you or if you will still and always be embarrassed by such overt displays of affection.

And you, my Colin, my laughing bundle of raw energy, I want to know how far your curiosity will take you; I need to know what is to become of that Cartesian mind of yours that already at the age of eight propounds scientific truths about which—to your great surprise—your papa, the Director of the Historial, knows nothing. Keep learning, my young one, keep surprising me; I promise I won't become impatient at your never-ending sentences; I'll suppress my sighs, and I'll diligently watch all your presentations. I hope you forgive me for abandoning our beloved museum. I hope you will no longer cry as you do now at the mention of this departure. You are everything I could have been, everything I would have wanted to be, and which I might have been if it were not for my childhood torn apart by mourning and absence.

And if it should happen that I must leave you, my children, know that I will have fought it with the very last of my energy. When we must part, we will have said everything that there is to say, and you and your children will not need to ask a stranger to tell you who your father was. Your mother will know exactly how to tell you all my little secrets, whether brilliant or dark. I want to hide nothing from you, and I will resist the temptation of wanting to appear extraordinary rather than simply human. I am a good father, I am convinced of that; I feel it, and the way you look at me tells me it is so. I promise to struggle to remain that way, to measure my words so as not to wound, to raise my voice only when I need to be heard at a greater distance. I have not insulted and will not insult anyone; not strangers, not you; not ever. The five years spent at the Historial were the years that saw you transition from the carefree innocence of early childhood to an apprenticeship of the world. You are now on the path that leads from bewildered discovery to the disappointments that haunt the world of adults. Your mother and I will try to prepare you for them, so that they will be neither cruel nor unbearable, and that you endure neither hate nor resentment. I don't want some Robert Comb making a toast to my son's memory. Yes, when it is time, we will be ready; we will have loved each other, and we will have no regrets—just one final breath, enough to say one more time "I love you."

There remains the terrifying question of knowing whether, beyond what I have hoped for you, beyond the

48

words, the tender gazes and the emotions, beyond what I write, you do not have in you the same seeds of my affliction. Will my genetic legacy pass on to you the torments it has inflicted upon me? As it is, I try to hide how it troubles me to see your worried faces. "Does it hurt? Where does it hurt? What sort of pain is it?" As no doctor has been able to give me a good answer, I have none to give you; and instead, in answer to your pained inquisition, in the end I find the strength to say: "it's nothing; it will pass."

***

This morning I went to the local office of the national health insurance administration. Having finally admitted defeat, I wanted to meet with a social worker so she could clear the brush from the tortuous path ahead of me that leads from paid employment to an official status of incapacitation. The texts on the subject are remarkably clear: One can work and be disabled, or be incapacitated and an invalid, or not work due to incapacitation yet not be an invalid, or be incapacitated and invalid and still work. . . . In other words, one may vary ad infinitum the possible combinations of incapacitation, disability and employment status. I had not imagined I needed to steel myself with courage and daring, and a sense of grasping at every opportunity offered, in order to attain the administrative equivalent of a holy grail; the process is a veritable medieval trial by ordeal. Between the clinic run by local government, the county administration for the handicapped and the national health insurance system, it is a wonder anyone who does not yet receive assistance can have any access at all to any public assistance. The irony, of course, is that if you are in need of assistance, that assistance is supposed to be where you are going to go looking for it.

The Péronne health system clinic is similar to so many other public buildings: old, dark and depressing. It has that certain quality of lighting one finds nowhere else, that yellowish and flickering miasma which hazes down from the neon tubes like hail from a stormy sky: instinctively, you bend your head down and scrunch up your shoulders. I waited my turn to be seated in one of six grey plastic chairs arranged in a semicircle along the back wall (the waiting room is circular), where we—the "socially secured" clients—mutter to ourselves as we wait.

It is my turn. Seated behind the counter, a heavyset woman with thick glasses glances at me with her left eye while the right daydreams out the window. "Yes?" Good morning, Madame. "Good morning, Monsieur." And I explain I would like to meet with a social worker to explore the possibilities of my dis— "Social Security Number?" Uh, 68 . . . "Ah, yes, Monsieur de Fonclare . . ." We delve into the details of my medical diagnosis, I present my concerns about my deteriorating health, my concerns for my work. In answer to one of her questions, I tell her I am—more or less—my own employer. She raises an eyebrow and quizzically peers at her computer screen, hoping to find some bit of data which might help. "Let me see . . . How is that you are your own employer? Aren't you a salaried employee?" she asks. I reply that I am the Director of the Historial. In that split-second, her stare morphs into a gaze of boundless pity. She hands me a piece of paper: "That's your social worker." I take the paper and extend my hand, which she shakes, clearly surprised. "I wish you much courage; yes, much courage," she intones sadly. I cross the waiting room, leave the building and climb into my car. I am devastated.

To be on the wrong side of the counter, to be the object of so much evident pity, feels like a knife twisted in my gut. To imagine that I will never work, that all professional contributions must cease, that I will have to leave to others— those who are not invalids—the duty of charting the course of the Historial . . . I am dumbfounded. So much emotion grips my heart; it creates a tsunami of tears that drowns out all reasoned thoughts and rips them to shreds. What is the use of returning to Railway Hollow Cemetery? What purpose is served by living and suffering in an all-too-early retirement? My retirement fund is well provisioned and will protect me from poverty, I cannot complain about that; but I am now dead—societally and professionally dead—and all that's left for me is to decide which hole I want to crawl into.

And yet, these are odd thoughts for one as tired as I am: I have so much difficulty getting up in the morning, I require so much energy just to shower, so much effort merely to tie my shoelaces, to suck in my gut and make believe everything is not-so-bad. How endless these days seem, the days on which I pretend to still be up to speed, to be genuinely interested in the new scenic treatment for the next exposition, or to the development of tourism for the Somme Valley. I am no longer lulled by the flattering looks of respect or admiration and, when I speak, the words betray nothing of the weariness that grows within me day after day, weekend after weekend. Once, I knew nothing but work; I saw time off as a necessary and mandated breathing space between projects; now I sigh with relief when a meeting is cancelled. I dream of work weeks that run from Tuesday morning to Thursday afternoon. If I allowed myself, I would awaken at eleven and return to bed at three. The one who for so long stifled the demands of his body would now give in to it at every opportunity just to have, if only one time, the satisfaction of being in harmony with myself.

***

Railway Hollow Cemetery on a July afternoon; I have struggled to get here. It is hot and the air is fragrant with pine resin as the summer breeze gently cascades pine needles to the ground. I feel well and I ponder.

Childhood: the golden days of racing toward no particular goal, of steep mountain paths, of our bodies sweating from exertion. Not one of us, in our eight years of existence on earth, has yet experienced such strong sensations. The sun was grinding the fragrances of thyme and sage into savage aromas; and from the wild oats, the wheat fields, the white dead-nettles and the compost, there arose cooler and more sedate perfumes. This was Combevin, the foothills of the Vercors, north of the Drome—almost Provence. The "almost" is due to the presence of abundant snow in winter and the absence of rosemary plants at any time of year. There, moreover, the Mistral has no name; it is just the north wind. There, separated by thirty-five years, is where my true happiness resided. It abandoned me one April or May evening on the coarse asphalt of the Village Hall parking lot. An hour after my father had informed us we were soon to forever leave this paradise, I stretched out on the ground and acted out, one more time, the death of Captain Nemo. I was, as usual, the hero of a play that invariably had only four characters, played by the only four children who lived in the village and who, scene after scene, invented what might have been called *The Green Paradise of Childhood Loves.*[7] Never was there asphalt so coarse, or death scene so outlandishly emoted. The tears that failed to gush that day have not flowed since then, either; they boiled and, if I had not been constantly vigilant, they would have boiled over into unbearable anger. Instead, I listened and learned, outstretched on the asphalt, under a merciless sun.

---

7   Refers to a line from Baudelaire's *Moesta et Errabunda* (Grieving and Wandering):
Mais le vert paradis des amours enfantines,
Les courses, les chansons, les baisers, les bouquets,
Les violons vibrant derrière les collines,

We left Combevin for Lambesc, a town near Aix-en-Provence. My father was a helicopter test pilot for Aérospatiale, which is now known as Eurocopter. I was about to turn ten when he was killed in a demonstration flight. It was during Easter break, and I was away at camp. I remember the return trip in a taxi whose driver spoke not a word. As I reflected on this surreal and early return home, the craziest suppositions flooded my thoughts. Death was the only hypothesis that kept resurfacing, even though it never occurred to me that it might be my father's death. My childhood abruptly ceased when the front door swung open to reveal my mother in tears. At that moment, Death entered my world wearing a mask: that of my mother's distorted face—the face of one who has just lost her lover, her friend, her brother; and yet, already visible in her eyes, the certainty that this new and terrible solitude was not sufficient justification for continuing to cry about her fate: To reach adulthood as best they could, her three children would need her to be strong.

I was obsessive about reading and in the family library I always sought out those stories whose heroes never died. Years passed, and the excellent student whom all the teachers praised cut himself off from the world. He remained a friend only to books and only the books remained faithful. I was abetted in this escape by Jules Verne whose *Mysterious Island*, which I obsessively read over and over, became my story: a forced confinement under the secret tutelage of a benevolent demiurge. Cyrus Smith and Captain Nemo were two reflections of my father's exalted image—the grandeur of physical courage and the nobility of the human spirit. I had to achieve the same perfection of being; I and some other self to become heroic and worthy of admiration—worthy of being my father.

Suddenly, after childhood there was adolescence, and Céline entered my life. Calm in all the ways I was tormented, full of common sense where I was filled with metaphysical question marks, she was radiant where I was dark. We were in 11th grade together. She was there because she had to be; I was there because I wanted to excel. She loved life, I feared it. I loved her immediately, passionately and unreasonably. I was seventeen, she eighteen. She showed me there is more to the world than just morbid nightmares; that it is good to be alive appreciating simple joys and a heart that is always light.

I matured. Day by day, from one morning to the next, I progressed toward the next stage of life. Adulthood? I do not know any adults. I know only children who play at being grown-ups and who forget that their warrior games stop being fun when the guns are no longer toys made of plastic. I have been acting like a grown-up for a long time now; too long, no doubt.

What remains of my father? Nothing, or almost nothing. Scattered memories, blurry images or blinding flashes; little bits of nothing which, placed end to end, make a whole— even if that whole is nothing much, even if the present too often mars the patina of old sorrows. That nothing much is what nonetheless remains palpable, tangible. I can feel its presence as it rises from deep within in me, as when the intonation of my voice has the resonance of my father's voice. And if there is this odd feeling that I am the guardian of so many unknown shadows, there is only one shadow that never leaves me, that knows how to stay out of the bright sunlight, the one which merges with the dark outline that follows me or stretches out on the sidewalk in front of me: It is the shadow of my father, whose hero I have always so much wanted to be.

His funeral service was held in one of the hangars of Aérospatiale in Marignan. There must have been over a thousand people in attendance. He was posthumously awarded the Aerospace Medal. A red velvet cushion had been placed on his coffin. The vision of this shiny medal on a scarlet background, in the middle of this huge crowd sniffling while we cried, has never left me. I have known the pain of being orphaned. I have seen a mother shattered by loss. I know the pain of mourning. 70,156,000 soldiers drafted; 9,442,000 dead. How many widows and orphans is that? Is it even reasonable to speak in the same breath of such a cataclysm and my own personal woes? Can you still call it mourning when an entire nation wears black? Yes, I know the pain of being orphaned, but I know nothing of collective grief, of mourning shared and carried high like a victory banner in the hope that, over there, on "the other side," they suffer just as much or more. And what can be said about an entire generation of sons without fathers, striving to measure up to one who "died for France," or about those who lower their heads in shame for being the offspring of a coward, a failure, a traitor? What can we say about these adults so poorly brought up because they had no one to mentor them, this generation that does not know how to love because they received so little love?

My best friend chose to end his life at the age of forty. He flung himself out the sixth story window of the office building where he worked. He is survived by his wife and two young girls. He did not seem to have any particular problems in life. I, at least, saw nothing other than that he worked a great deal. Too much was expected of him at work, and it is only after he had crashed into the pavement of the parking lot that it was understood what "too much" meant. I was ready to raise hell, to bring this to public attention, to shout on the rooftops that he was one of these innocent victims of "the workplace mentality" where "competition" is synonymous with hand-to-hand combat and "the market" is another name for battlefield. I eventually subdued my anger, and all I can feel now is immense sadness. The body I saw at the morgue wasn't his anymore. The face on the cadaver had nothing in common with that of my friend, despite all of the mortician's expertise and effort. He did not even seem dead: He looked like someone other than himself, someone I did not even know. I found this to be deeply disturbing. I had prepared myself for a morbid confrontation with reality; I was even impatient to get it over with, as I thought this might be an important step—perhaps a decisive step—towards accepting the unimaginable. It did not happen. At the Père Lachaise Cemetery, the ceremony before the cremation of his body was heart-wrenching: There were so many people in tears, so many people who seemed genuinely affected by this loss. At first, the depth of emotion surprised me; but, as I began to remember the kind of person he had been, surprise gave way to respect. The person being eulogized was indeed the person I had known, this dearest friend, this more-than-brother. I shall never again know such unspoken understanding, such mutual affection that needs no words to be expressed, a communion that shuns the hyperbole of words in favor of a reserved and mutual honesty. A friend; I have lost a friend.

In July of 1916 how many families did the mayor of Accrington plunge into despair? Seven hundred of his fellow citizens took part in the Somme Offensive of July 1st. Two hundred and thirty-five of them were killed and three hundred and fifty more were wounded in the just the first hour. How many "brothers in arms," how many friends lost each other forever in that one hour? And for those who survived the war, there was the long trip to the gaily-decorated or mourning-draped facades of home. One can easily imagine that, for many, the joyful celebrations of victory may have left a rather bitter aftertaste.

Violent thoughts such as these have worn me down and tainted my outlook on daily life; the endlessly repeated choruses of invisible tears have wounded me so thoroughly I thought they had changed me forever. I am surprised to discover today that this has not been the case: I am still who I used to be. Paradoxically, it is the vision of these piles of cadavers, those noseless faces, those missing limbs, those white bones on the black earth, and the departed forty-something friends who have drawn me closer to life. Now, if I mourn, I do so silently; and that silence is the silence of a child mourning a dead father, of a wife overcoming the horror of an unrecognizable face, of flowering green parks dotted with white steles. Little by little, as I prepare for my own departure, I divest myself of all trappings: I will take off the costume of Museum Director in order to put on the one belonging to Guillaume de Fonclare—just Guillaume. This gradual transition will not tear me apart, for it no longer tortures me; I will let sleeping ghosts sleep in peace and, in measured steps, I will go forward towards a new world, hoping that my new America will offer me everything I seek. My children will grow up while we spend weekends and vacations together, and the one I love will sustain me just as she has done all along. For my part, I shall try not to grow too old too quickly; and to be alone, peacefully alone, when I need to hide my pain.

Railway Hollow Cemetery on a July afternoon; I daydream.

***

You, horrid war, you who have taken my beloved from me and given me in his place nothing but tears, you have never wanted me to be happy.

You made me throw away the dress of a wife and don instead the wide veil of the pitiful widow. Why? Were you jealous of our happiness?

And you, beloved husband, at thirty-eight you left your wife to avenge the homeland but also left me virtually without hope. At thirty-nine, after a year of torment, you left me—alas for all time—with a broken heart.

Now, my only consolation is to kneel on this icy stone. Adieu, dear husband. I will cry for you the rest of my life.

Write as I might, struggle as I might to find the exact words, the perfect sentence that communicates everything, I come up with nothing that expresses grief more movingly than those few lines from a gravestone. The stone is in Room 2 of the Historial in a glass showcase. It is just to the right of another glass case, this one containing a black dress, black hat and black veil. Death was this woman's rival—It always has the last word in all things, and War is its accomplice. What more is there to say? That text instructs us at so many levels that, to parse it out properly, I might fill a dozen pages; but it is in its utter simplicity that it says everything there is to say. I would have liked to be able to do the same.

Yesterday, I finally came to the decision to put my affairs in order: after I return from vacation, after this summer—in the winter or early spring perhaps—I will begin the process of a transition to decreasing activity and stopping work. The dozens of pages I have written will have served no other purpose than to bring me to this point: I thought I was disillusioned and bitter; I am not. As I read again the text of that tombstone, that poem of magnificent love and dignity, I discovered new meaning to loss and mourning. Loss is irreparable and mourning begins with precisely that realization: What is gone will not come back.

When, in the process of losing control of my body I lose work or social acceptance or indeed any life-activity, it is a huge portion of my life that I leave and must abandon forever.

The only choice left to me, then, is to either moan or agree to live with this loss. I must learn to believe in myself and not tie my sense of self to that societal self, the Director of the Historial. Soon, the Director will have a different name and he may feel haunted by my ghost. He will know that what the Historial staff and I built together really belongs only to us; but he will also know that, later on, he will encounter the staff on new ground. I, on the other hand, will have lost them; a little bit more with each passing year, and eventually, I will lose them and be lost to them entirely. The Director of the Historial will be different, but I, I will still exist. Divesting myself of my Director's uniform will not leave me naked: I will wear my own clothes and learn to be, and love being.

Of The Great War, I take with me faces and smiles. The faces of those who kept me company, faces both known and unfamiliar, and smiles of those who cared for me and are no longer here. A procession of shadows will mark a trail for me towards that other night. There, I will rest, contented. After this much pain, such a night seems peaceful—a liberation from woe. But that does not mean I am in a hurry to get there; rather, I go there calmly while savoring life. I owe them at least that.

It was the museum that saved me: it saved me from depression, from despair. It was the museum which lit the small spark in me that I still have time to nurture into a fire. Through the suffering of those multitudes, I learned to both accept and respect my own pain. There is no moral lesson in that; merely a statement of fact. I did not silence my pain because I encountered more or deeper suffering. Indeed not; my pain is here and it is in no way diminished. There is no such thing as one suffering being greater than any other. The museum taught me modesty, courage, humility, forgiveness of self and others, and hope. It was there that I began to build the me I shall become; it was there that I learned what it means to be human, to fully be a man—just a man.

For the past five years, my body has been in the red zone, that zone where destruction and hope fight each other. I am unable to tell at what precise moment I crossed the borders, nor even describe exactly what those limits were. Was it first one single cell which began to rebel and rallied thousands of its fellow cells as partisans in the rebellion? Or was it deep in the recesses of my amygdala that a sleeping reptile awoke from a bad dream and shook itself so violently that it turned my neurons inside out and unsheathed my nervous system? Even if I am told it is impossible to rebuild, I will rebuild. I will rebuild a life that can plausibly be lived in this diseased body. It has been dragging me around for so long, it is about time I did some dragging of my own; but I will do so wisely, at a pace it is willing to accept. I'll learn to listen when it complains, try to understand its pains and heal them or calm them as best I can. We will go forward, limping here and there, paying no attention to taunts or sarcastic remarks. One foot in front of the other, we will go forward together towards that "over there" which I have learned to no longer fear. More importantly, I will have learned how to live inside my own skin.

***

ACKNOWLEDGMENTS

If I were to thank all those who, in one way or another, have contributed to the existence of this narrative, either as to content or form, the acknowledgements would take up two hundred pages. I think back to my teachers who were the first to make me love the written word: Mademoiselle Fournier, Madame Testut, Monsieur Boulièche, Monsieur Paul and so many others who never knew what they had done for me. I haven't forgotten.

Then there are those who guided my pen, who encouraged me and sustained (in every sense of those words) among whom I count Princesse Grenadine, the indispensable Mylène and the essential Roxane, my Singular Tyrant(s), Ninon and the invisible Dissolved.

Finally, I wish to express my gratitude towards those who surround me daily, and whose kindness brightens every one of my days. Thank you, therefore, to Amèlie, Francois, Yves, Hélène, Cathy, Christine, Marie-Luz, Nathalie, Alain, Evelyne, Dawn, Dominique, (the other) Yves, Frédéric and Frédérick, Mickaël, Vincent, Séverine, Emilie, Nathalie, Cécile, Clotilde, Karine, Steve, Christine, Catherine, Céline, Bernadette, Julie, Emilie, Gérard, Angèle, Laurent, André, Sébastien, Caroline and Marie-Pascale, as well as Philippe and Pierre for the trust they placed in me.

I also dedicate this book to my big sister in writing. She knows who she is and will recognize herself in these pages.

TRANSLATOR'S AFTERWORD

"We're all of us sentenced to solitary confinement, inside our own skins, for life."
—Val Xavier in *Orpheus Descending,*
Tennessee Williams

À New York, le 1ᵉʳ Septembre 2013
Cher Monsieur de Fonclare,

The translation you hold in your hands almost never happened and, once it did happen, it almost had a very different title. Indeed, In My Skin is already the title of an Australian book and a French movie but even without those potential complications, it struck me as an inappropriately literal translation of your *Dans Ma Peau*. From a purely semantic point of view, the culturally equivalent and more exact expression would have been "In My Shoes." Interestingly enough Ana Mihailescu, the Romanian translator of your work, may have encountered similar concerns as she chose to entitle her translation *Prizonier în propriul corp, A Prisoner In My Own Body.*

I abandoned the metaphor of walking in someone else's shoes as equally incomplete; but only gave myself permission to do so when I remembered the line by Val Xavier in Tennessee Williams' *Orpheus Descending* about living out our lives in solitary confinement inside our own skins. In addition to trading on the authority of Tennessee Williams, this solution had the added benefit of incorporating, if only by allusion, the notion of the prison of one's body, a notion which Mihailescu had—in my opinion so aptly—imparted to her translation, even if such an adaptation may initially have been the result of the impossibility of a literal translation. It is

63

comforting to note that, sometimes, the task of the translator includes welcoming or giving in to "happy accidents" and synchronicities.

That explains the title. As to the present translation almost not existing (at least at this time) it needs to be said that I began the project of translating your *récit* in early July 2013, thinking there would be plenty of time to have an entirely polished tiny gem, as closely resembling your original as I could fashion it, finished in time to present to publishers for 2014, the 100th anniversary year of the start of World War I. Quite ironically, my plans were rudely interrupted by the flare-up of an old syndrome, one of those ailments "of unknown etiology" you describe. Fortunately for me, my syndrome has never reached the severity or intensity of the one you have experienced and continue to battle. While I am no closer to putting a name on my own syndrome, I have been fortunate enough to discover, through a combination of Western and alternative medicinal traditions, certain strategies which keep the symptoms at bay—or at least under control for long stretches of time. It is my sincere hope such a breakthrough is found for you. I attached no cosmic significance to the timing of this flare-up other than, perhaps, as yet another interesting real-world example of synchronicity: causally unrelated events occurring in a proximal time-space.

As expected, the night in the Emergency Room in a hospital in Queens, New York, generated no new insight into my condition; It did, however, provide an ironic contrast between my pre-Affordable Care Act state of temporary uninsured-ness and your complaints about what happens to be (according to the World Health Organization at least) one of the best public health insurance systems in the world.

More than the interesting synchronicity or the telling ironies, your text has a deep personal resonance for me. I first discovered the book while researching background material for a historical fiction piece based upon the lives of two grandfathers, both of them veterans of World War I. The name of the Historial of Péronne and its dedicated curator kept cropping up as I dug for pictures and firsthand accounts on the Internet. I eventually purchased the book and of course read it not merely in one sitting but, metaphorically at least, in one breath: Your great-grandfather might have fought alongside one of my own grandfathers. The dizzying numbers you rattle off have a corollary that we rarely remember: the larger the number, the higher the probability that "unlikely occurrences" will in fact occur.

My two grandfathers' lives intersected so many times before their children ever met and married, it would be easy to suggest that the hand of destiny was at work (or at play). But the reality is so much simpler and requires no metaphysical or magical explanation: the currents of history at the onset of the 20th century were so broad, so strong, and ran so deep as to sweep up everything and everyone and wash them up on the shores of specific times and places of convergence; you talk about tsunamis of emotion and thought. The image also applies to all the "small stories" that make up history.

Both grandfathers were amateur historians as well as master storytellers. They could describe the battle of Crécy or Hastings, or indeed any significant moment of history, as if they had been there at the right hand of the King—except that they had the added advantage of distance and history, and could tell you the precise moment the King made a costly, sometimes fatal, mistake.

Both grandfathers filled my childhood with vivid accounts of "World History's Greatest Moments." And yet, never once did they speak about their part in World War I. As a child, I never understood how someone could describe a battle of 1346 as if he had been there, but never speak about October 7th, 1916 when—as far as I have been able to determine—he was only a few hundred yards across no-man's land from the trench which sheltered an Austrian Corporal by the name of Adolph Hitler. For all anyone knows, my grandfather could have been the one who wounded Hitler in the leg on that day. But such thoughts are the romantic wonderings of a child who cannot possibly know what his grandfathers don't want him to know. When I read your line *"...their stories have never been heard because they never said a word,"* I nodded in recognition and, I must confess, the tears welled up.

I am who and what I am today in large part thanks to my grandfathers; and they were who and what they were, and the world they left me is what it is, in large part because of World War I. More than any century that preceded it, the 20th century incarnated the double-edged sword of civilization: the human ability to display infinite kindness and nobility of spirit as well as to commit unspeakable and unimaginable acts of barbarism. As we approach the 100th anniversary of the onset of World War I, we would do well to remember—and live by—the Historial's mission statement as you expressed it: we need to *"celebrate the human being, the breadth of his suffering and the unfathomable depth of his stupidity."*

Merci, Monsieur de Fonclare.

Bien Sincèrement,
Yves Cloarec

Yves Cloarec lectures in European Civilization, English, and French at the City University of New York's Queens College campus, where he is a candidate for the MFA in Creative Writing and Literary Translation. He also still directs NextWave Office Systems, the computer consulting and database management software design company that he founded in 1994. Before that, he worked for the French government in its Departments of Tourism and Economic Development; and as a translator and interpreter for international government and non-government agencies on both sides of the Atlantic. He was born in Martinique, French West Indies; he holds a French Baccalauréat degree, and a Bachelor's in Political Science and English from Columbia University. He is currently studying Breton, the language of his ancestors, and planning to translate some of its previously untranslated medieval texts.